LEARNING ADVENTURES
IN MATH
Grades 1–2

By the Staff of Score@Kaplan

Foreword by Alan Tripp

Simon & Schuster

**This series is dedicated to our
Score@Kaplan parents and children—
thank you for making these books possible.**

Published by
Kaplan Educational Centers and Simon & Schuster
1230 Avenue of the Americas
New York, NY 10020

Special thanks to: Elissa Grayer, Doreen Beauregard, Julie Schmidt, Rebecca Geller
Schwartz, Linda Lott, Janet Cassidy, Marlene Greil, Nancy McDonald, Sarah Jane
Bryan, Chris Wilsdon, Janet Montal, Jeannette Sanderson, David Stienecker, Dan
Greenberg, Kathy Wilmore, Dorrie Berkowitz, Brent Gallenberger, and Molly Walsh

Head Coach and General Manager, Score@Kaplan: Alan Tripp
President, Score@Kaplan: Robert L. Waldron
Series Content and Development: Mega-Books
Project Editor: Mary Pearce
Production Editor: Donna Mackay, Graphic Circle Inc.
Art Director: Elana Goren-Totino
Illustrators: Rick Brown, Ryan Brown, Sandy Forrest, Larry Nolte,
Evan Polenghi, Fred Schrier, Peter Spacek, Arnie Ten
Cover Design: Cheung Tai
Cover Photograph: Michael Britto

Manufactured in the United States of America
Published Simultaneously in Canada

January 1998
10 9 8 7 6 5 4 3 2 1

ISBN:0-684-84427-3

Contents

Grade One

Grade Two

Dear Parents,

Your child's success in school is important to you, and at Score@Kaplan we are always pleased when the kids who attend our educational centers do well on their report cards. But what we really want for our kids is not just good grades. We also want everything that good grades are supposed to represent:

- We want our kids to master the key communication systems that make civilization possible: language (spoken and written), math, the visual arts, and music.
- We want them to build their critical-thinking skills so they can understand, appreciate, and improve their world.
- We want them to continually increase their knowledge and to value learning as the key to a happy, successful life.
- We want them to always do their best, to persist when challenged, to be a force for good, and to help others whenever they can.

These are ambitious goals, but our children deserve no less. We at Score@Kaplan have already helped thousands of children across the country in our centers, and we hope this series of books for children in first through sixth grades will reach many more households.

Simple Principles

We owe the remarkable success of Score@Kaplan to a few simple principles. This book was developed with these principles in mind.

- We expect every child to succeed.
- We make it possible for every child to succeed.
- We reinforce every instance of success, no matter how small.

Assessing Your Child

One helpful approach in assessing your child's skills is to ask yourself the following questions.

- How much is my child reading? At what level of difficulty?
- Has my child mastered appropriate language arts skills, such as spelling, grammar, and syntax?
- Does my child have the ability to express appropriately complex thoughts when speaking or writing?
- Does my child demonstrate mastery of all age-appropriate math skills, such as mastery of addition and subtraction facts, multiplication tables, division rules, and so on?

These questions are a good starting place and may give you new insights into your child's academic situation.

What's Going on at School

Parents will always need to monitor the situation at school and take responsibility for their child's learning. You should find out what your child should be learning at each grade level and match that against what your child actually learns.

The activity pages in *Learning Adventures* were developed using the standards developed by the professional teachers associations. As your child explores the activities in *Learning Adventures*, you might find that a particular concept hasn't been taught in school or hasn't yet been mastered by your child. This presents a great opportunity for both of you. Together you can learn something new.

Encouraging Your Child to Learn at Home

This book is full of fun learning activities you can do with your child to build understanding of key concepts in language arts, math, and science. Most activities are designed for your child to do independently. But that doesn't mean that you can't work on them together or invite your child to share the work with you. As you help your child learn, please bear in mind the following observations drawn from experience in our centers:

- Positive reinforcement is the key. Try to maintain a ratio of at least five positive remarks to every negative one.
- All praise must be genuine. Try praises such as: "That was a good try," "You got this part of it right," or "I'm proud of you for doing your best, even though it was hard."
- When a child gets stuck, giving the answer is often not the most efficient way to help. Ask open-ended questions, or rephrase the problem.
- Remember to be patient and supportive. Children need to learn that hard work pays off.

There's More to Life Than Academic Learning

Most parents recognize that academic excellence is just one of the many things they would like to ensure for their children. At Score@Kaplan, we are committed to developing the whole child. These books are designed to emphasize academic skills and critical thinking, as well as provide an opportunity for positive reinforcement and encouragement from you, the parent.

We wish you a successful and rewarding experience as you and your child embark upon this learning adventure together.

Alan Tripp
General Manager
Score@Kaplan

Dear Kids,

This is your very own book of Learning Adventures.
It has puzzles, games, riddles, and lots of other fun things for
you to do.
You can do the activities alone.
Or you can share them with your family and friends.

If you get stuck on something, look for the Score Coaches.
They will help you.
You can check the answers on pages 65–70, too.

We know you will do a great job.
That's why we have a special puzzle inside.
After you do three or four pages, you'll see a puzzle piece.
Cut it out.
Then glue it or tape it in place on page 64.
When you are done with the book, the puzzle will be done, too.
Then you'll find a secret message from us.

Go for it!

Your Coaches at Score

Count On You!

**You are full of numbers!
Count on you.
Then write how many you have on the line.**

1. The number of eyes you have _TWO_

2. The number of things you have on that are blue

_____

3. The number of fingers and toes you have all

together _____

4. The number of brothers and sisters you have_____

5. The number of missing teeth you have _____

6. The number of bandages you are wearing right

now _____

7. The number of seconds you can hold your breath

_____

8. The number of pairs of shoes in your closet

_____

Around the House: Count on your family.

The number of fingers_____

The number of legs (including pets) _____

The number of ears_____

The number of pairs of glasses_____

NAME _____

Helmet Help

The football team washed their helmets.
Some numbers came off!
Help the team.
Write in the missing numbers.
One is done for you.

The helmets are in number order. You have to count by ones.

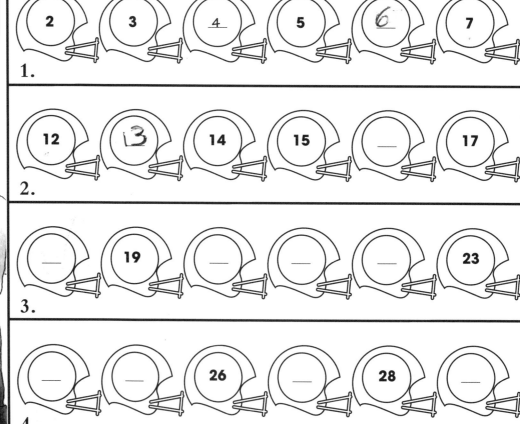

1. 2 3 4 5 6 7

2. 12 13 14 15 ___ 17

3. ___ 19 ___ ___ ___ 23

4. ___ ___ 26 ___ 28 ___

Around the House: There are lots of things to count in your house. Try counting cups, doors, or beds!

NAME_____

Number Toss 3 3 3 3 3

9
6 6 9

Here's how to play Number Toss:

1. Toss a paper clip onto the game board. Write the number you land on on another piece of paper.
2. Toss again. Write down that number.
3. Put the numbers together to make a 2-digit number. Make the biggest number you can.
4. Fill in the chart with your number.
5. Play Number Toss five times.

> Here's a hint! Use the bigger number in the tens place.

	tens	ones	number
1	8	4	5
2		9	6
3			
4			
5			

0	1		
2	3 3 3		
4	5	6	7
	8	9	

Around the House: Try playing this game with a friend. Who can make the biggest number?

NAME _____

Froggy Fun

Help the frogs play leapfrog.
Each frog is skip counting and hopping from pad to pad.
Figure out the pattern.
Then skip count and write the numbers that come next on the pads.

Skip count and write the numbers for each frog.

Around the House: Look for objects in your house to skip count.

4

Grade 1

NAME_____

Math Machine

Put each number into the machine.
Then follow the directions.
Write each answer in the correct shape at the
bottom of the machine.
One is done for you.

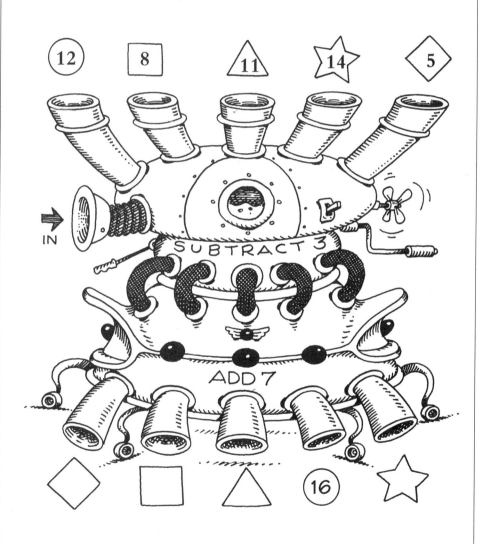

Don't forget to
write down your
answers for
each section of
the machine on
another piece
of paper.

Now, start
your puzzle.
Glue or tape
this piece in
place on
page 64.

Check Yourself: Were the answers in order from
smallest to biggest?

NAME _____

Find the Partners

Help the children find their partners.
Read each problem.
Find the partner who has the right number of marbles.
Write the partner's name on the line.

Use the number line to count on if you like.

Greg   Ian   Eloise

Zoe

1. Sally has 6 marbles. She needs 13 all together.
   Who should be her partner?_____

2. Justin has 3 marbles. He needs 16 all together.
   Who should be his partner? _____

3. Talia has 10 marbles. She needs 18 all together.
   Who should be her partner?_____

4. Joshua has 7 marbles. He needs 16 all together.
   Who should be his partner? _____

Check Yourself: Is there a girl and a boy in each pair?

NAME_____

Go Figure

Add the numbers in each problem.
Then look at the code.
Use your answers to find the secret message.
One is done for you.

CODE								
M	I	A	H	F	U	T	S	N
38	56	69	78	79	83	89	94	99

$$\begin{array}{r} 12 \\ + 26 \\ \hline 38 \end{array}\qquad \begin{array}{r} 43 \\ + 26 \\ \hline \end{array}\qquad \begin{array}{r} 72 \\ + 17 \\ \hline \end{array}\qquad \begin{array}{r} 45 \\ + 33 \\ \hline \end{array}$$

[M] [ ] [ ] [ ]

$$\begin{array}{r} 31 \\ + 25 \\ \hline \end{array}\qquad \begin{array}{r} 84 \\ + 10 \\ \hline \end{array}$$

[ ] [ ]

$$\begin{array}{r} 27 \\ + 52 \\ \hline \end{array}\qquad \begin{array}{r} 52 \\ + 31 \\ \hline \end{array}\qquad \begin{array}{r} 79 \\ + 20 \\ \hline \end{array}$$

[ ] [ ] [ ]

First add the numbers in the ones place. Then add the numbers in the tens place.

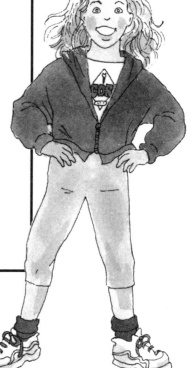

Check Yourself: Did you use each letter once?
Does the message make sense?

NAME

Subtraction Road

Can you get to the end of the road?
Do the first problem.
Then lightly color that part of the road.
Keep going until the whole road is colored.

Remember: when you subtract, subtract the numbers in the ones place first.

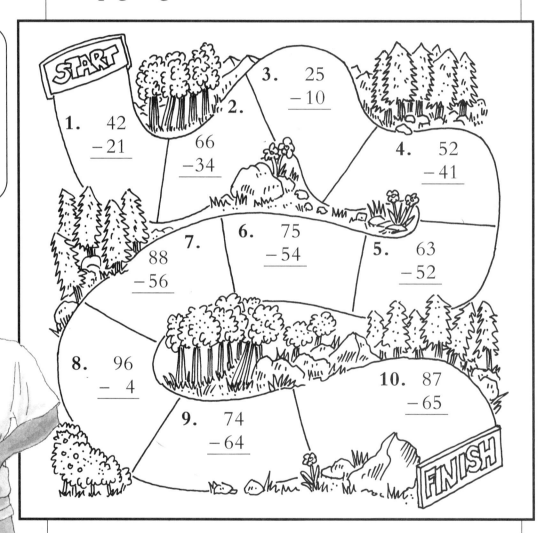

Check Yourself: You can use addition to check your subtraction. Add the answer to the number you took away. The answer should be the number you started with.

NAME_____

Go Fish!

Use addition to help you subtract.
Do each problem. Write the missing number.
The first one is done for you.

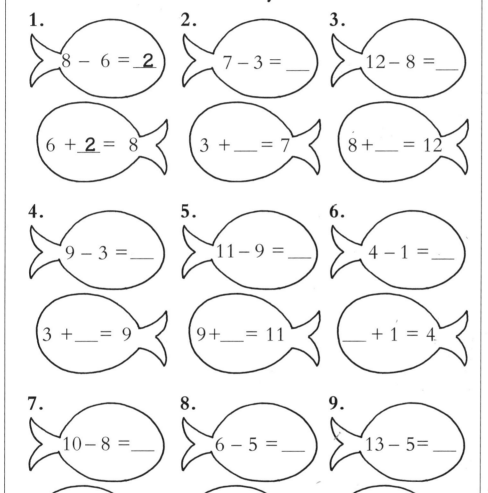

1.
$8 - 6 = \underline{2}$

$6 + \underline{2} = 8$

2.
$7 - 3 = \underline{}$

$3 + \underline{} = 7$

3.
$12 - 8 = \underline{}$

$8 + \underline{} = 12$

4.
$9 - 3 = \underline{}$

$3 + \underline{} = 9$

5.
$11 - 9 = \underline{}$

$9 + \underline{} = 11$

6.
$4 - 1 = \underline{}$

$\underline{} + 1 = 4$

7.
$10 - 8 = \underline{}$

$\underline{} + 8 = 10$

8.
$6 - 5 = \underline{}$

$5 + \underline{} = 6$

9.
$13 - 5 = \underline{}$

$5 + \underline{} = 13$

Addition and
subtraction are
opposites.
Use the
missing number
to help you
solve the
subtraction.

Check Yourself: Does the same number work in
both sentences? If it does, you subtracted right! (If not,
try again.)

NAME _____

Bug Count

Marla counts the insects at the museum.
Find out how many she has.
Write an addition sentence to show how to
add the sets of insects.
The first one is done for you.

Did you notice?
The sets in each
problems are
the same.
That means you
can use repeated
addition.

Great counting!
Now find the
place for the
puzzle piece on
page 64. Glue or
tape it in place.

1.

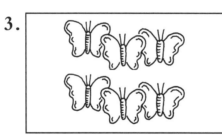

How many ladybugs?

$3 + 3 + 3 = 9$

2.

How many beetles?

_____

3.

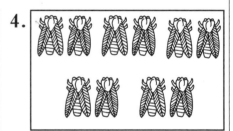

How many butterflies?

_____

4.

How many moths?

_____

5.

How many grasshoppers? _____

Check Yourself: After you add, count and see if
you are right!

NAME_____

What's the Time?

Read the time on each clock.
Then read each question.
Write the letter of the correct clock on the line.
The first one is done for you.

A.   B.   C.   D.

E.   F.   G.

1. Which clock shows 8:00? __E__

2. Which clock shows 7 o'clock?_____

3. Which two clocks show the same time?

    _____and_____

4. What time does clock F show?_____

5. What time does clock G show?_____

Make this clock show your favorite time of day. Then write a sentence that tells why it is your favorite time.

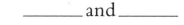

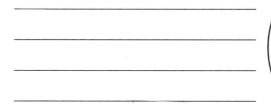

Remember, the small hand shows the hour. And when the large hand points to the 6, it is 30 minutes past the hour.

Grade 1

11

NAME _____

Coin Count

Help the children count their money.
Count each child's money.
Write the amount on the line.

Amy _____

Jenny _____

Tad _____

Who has the most money? _____

12

NAME_____

Tag Sale

Look at the stuff you can get at the tag sale.
You have $1.00. Circle 3 items you could buy.
Then answer the questions below.

To figure out your change, add up what you spent in all. Then subtract that sum from how much money you have.

Now figure out where to put this puzzle piece on page 64. Glue or tape it in place.

How much did you spend?

_____ + _____ + _____ = _____

How much change will you get back?

$1.00 − _____ = _____

Check Yourself: Go back and check your addition.
Did you add the prices of everything you picked? Did
you line up the tens and ones?

NAME _____

What's It Like Out?

When it is 32°F or colder, water freezes, and it will snow instead of rain.
A classroom is kept at about 70°F. If the temperature goes higher, it's too hot.

Look at the pictures.
How warm or cold is it in each one?
Draw a line to match each picture with the closest temperature on a thermometer.

 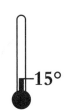

15°

1. Melissa cools off at the beach today.

 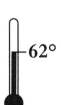

62°

2. Raul needs just a light jacket today.

90°

3. Midori needs her winter jacket, but she can't go skating today.

35°

4. Ted can build a snowman today.

NAME

Measure Up

Cut out the ruler.
Then read each question.
Use your ruler to help you answer it.
Write about how many inches each thing is.
(You don't have to be exact.)
The first one is done for you.

1. About how wide is this book?

   about 8 inches

2. About how long is this book?

   _____

3. About how long is your pencil?

   _____

4. About how long is your nose?

   _____

5. Smile! How wide can you smile?

   _____

6. Measure your foot. About how long is it?

   _____

7. Measure a grown-up's foot. About how long is it?

   _____

8. Stand against a wall. Mark the spot. How tall are you in inches?

   _____

This is an *inch*.
12 inches is called 1 *foot*.

⌞____⌟
1 inch

1 inch

2 inches

3 inches

4 inches

5 inches

6 inches

NAME ______________________________

Centimeter Sense

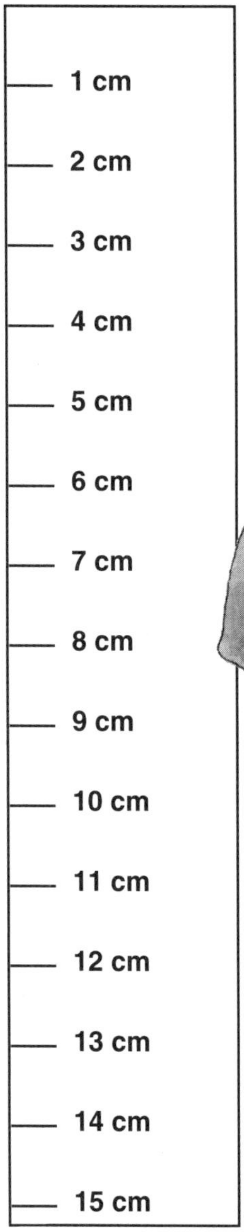
1 cm
2 cm
3 cm
4 cm
5 cm
6 cm
7 cm
8 cm
9 cm
10 cm
11 cm
12 cm
13 cm
14 cm
15 cm

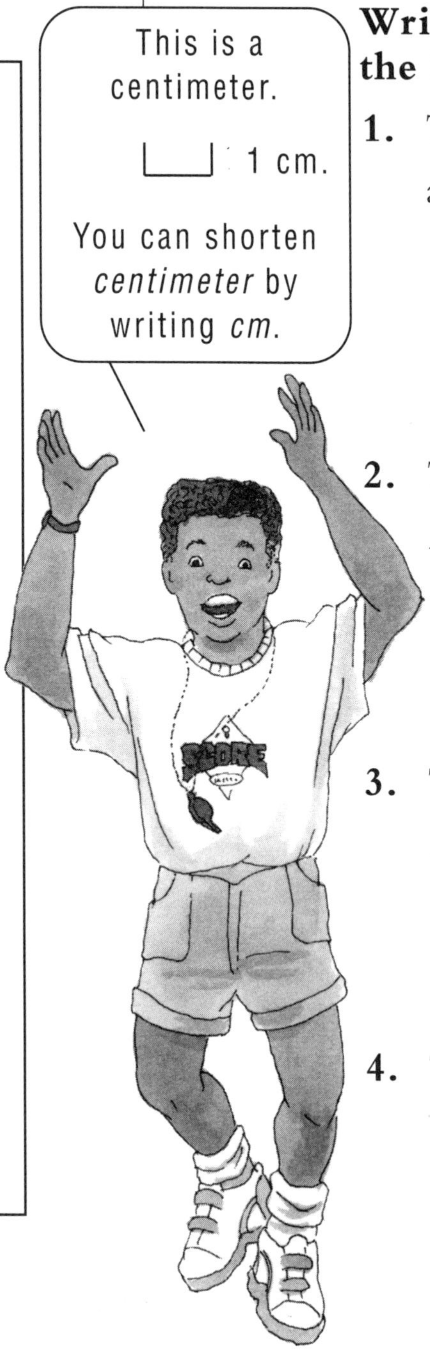
This is a centimeter.
1 cm.
You can shorten *centimeter* by writing *cm*.

Turn over the ruler you cut out. Look at the centimeter ruler. Use it to measure the things on this page. Write each measurement on the line.

1. The pencil is __1__ centimeter wide and ____ centimeters long.

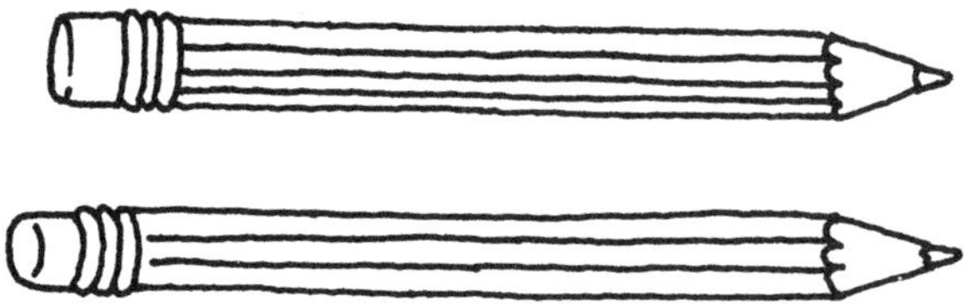

2. The crayon is ____ cm wide and ____ cm long.

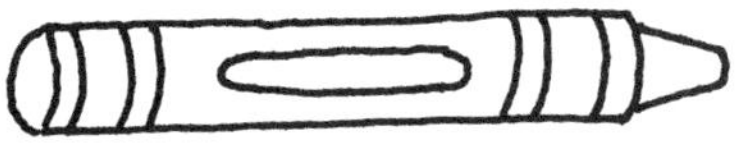

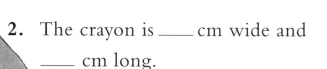

3. The paper clip is ____ cm wide and ____ cm long.

4. The eraser is ____ cm wide and ____ cm long.

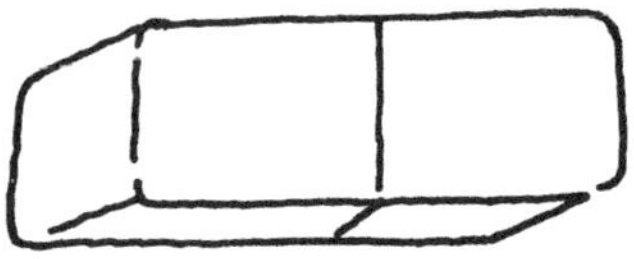

NAME_____

How Heavy?

Look at the objects.
Number them from 1 to 4 to put them in order from lightest to heaviest.
Then write a word or words to complete each sentence below.

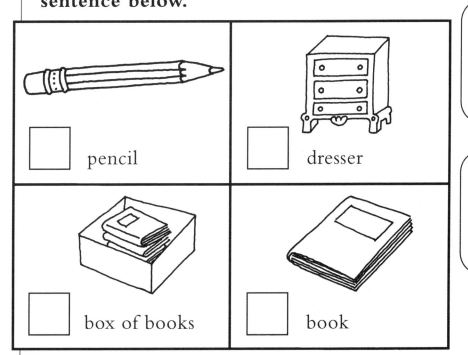

pencil

dresser

box of books

book

These items weigh about 1 pound.

Then these must weigh more than 1 pound.

1. The dresser weighs more than the_____,
   the _____ , and the_____ .

2. The _____ weighs less than one book.

3. The box of books weighs more than the
   _____ and the _____ .

4. The_____ weighs more than the pencil
   and less than the box of books.

NAME _____

Shape Hunt

Look at the picture.
Get out your crayons.
Follow the directions below.

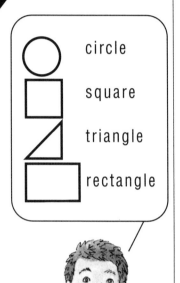

circle

square

triangle

rectangle

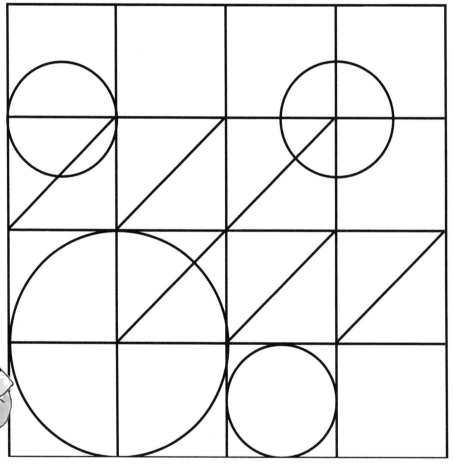

1. Find 4 circles. Color them red.
2. Find 6 triangles. Color them green.
3. Find 4 rectangles. Color them yellow.
4. Find 1 square. Color it blue.

Around the House: Look for shapes in your bedroom. Draw a picture of each shape you find.

Match Up

**Look at the solid shapes.
Read the directions next to each one.
Change the shape into a real object.
Then color each picture.**

Look around you. These shapes are everywhere.

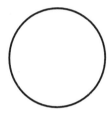 Make the *sphere* into a beach ball.

Make the *cone* into an ice cream cone.

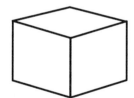 Make the *cube* into a TV.

Make the *cylinder* into a soup can.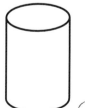

Now use your shape skills to put the puzzle piece in place on page 64. Tape or glue it in place.

Around the House: Have a shape hunt. See how many of these solid shapes you can find in your house in 10 minutes.

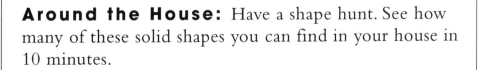

19

NAME _____

Riddle Fun

Can you solve the riddle?
Read each clue.
Circle the right shape.
Then put the letters in order on the answer lines.

Riddle: What has teeth but cannot bite?
Answer: ____ ____ ____ ____ ____
           1   2   3   4   5

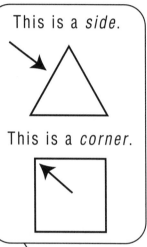
This is a *side*.

This is a *corner*.

1. This shape has no corners and no sides.

C   A   R   K

2. This shape has 4 sides and 4 corners.

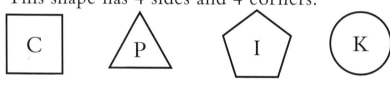

C   P   I   K

3. This shape has 3 sides.

S   O   F   R

4. This shape is like a square. But 2 sides are longer than the other 2 sides.

V   E   M   S

5. This shape has 5 corners.

W   B   I   P

NAME_____

Make a Necklace

Finish these necklaces.
Decide what comes next in each pattern.
Draw the next 3 beads in the pattern.
The first one shows you how.

1.

2.

3.

4.

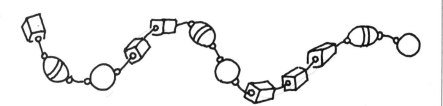

Look at the way
each item is alike
or different from
the ones next
to it.

Nice job!
It's time! Glue or
tape this piece in
place on page 64.

Around the House: Look for patterns in the
drapes, the wallpaper, the floors, and other places at your
house. Draw the pattern you find that you like best.

Grade 1

21

NAME _____

Cake Cuts

The baker divided these cakes into pieces. He wanted the pieces in each cake to be equal.
But he made one mistake in each row.
Put an X on the cake that does not show equal parts.

Don't forget to look at all four shapes in each row.

1.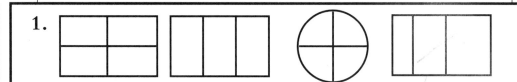

2.

3.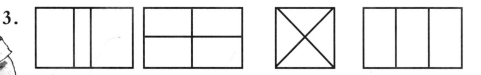

4.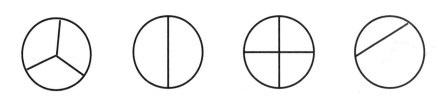

Check Yourself: Look again. If the parts are equal, each part is the same size as the others.

Around the House: Look around your house. Find something that is divided into equal parts. (Hint: look at the windows.) How many equal parts are there?

NAME_____

Snack Time

Ezra wants to share some snacks with his
friends.
Read each sentence.
Look at the pictures.
Circle the picture that answers the question.

A *whole* cake is in
one piece.
A cake divided in
half has two equal
pieces.
A cake divided into
thirds has three
equal pieces.
A cake divided into
fourths has four
equal pieces.

1. Three children want a piece of his cookie.
   Which cookie is divided into thirds?

2. Two children want a piece of his banana.
   Which banana is divided into halves?

3. Four children want a piece of his apple.
   Which apple is divided into fourths?

4. Ezra likes to eat his tart alone.
   Which tart is whole?

Around the House: Find a snack that you can
divide and share with a friend. Divide it in half, thirds,
or fourths.

NAME _____

Pet Power

The kids in the Pet Club made this graph.
It shows how many pets they have.
Read the graph.
Use the graph to answer the questions below.

Look down the left side of the graph to read the names of the pets. Count the pictures to see how many there are of each pet.

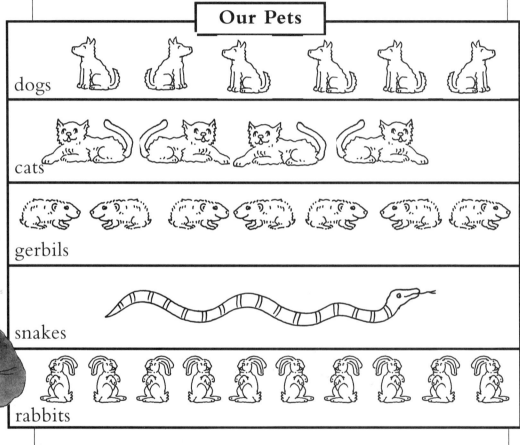

Our Pets

dogs

cats

gerbils

snakes

rabbits

1. How many of the pets are gerbils? _____

2. What pet do members have the most of? _____

3. Are there more dogs or cats? _____

4. What pet does only 1 member have? _____

5. A new member joined the club. She has a cat.
   Add it to the graph.

24

Grade 1

NAME_____

Sport Sort

Test your sports smarts.
Look at the objects in each box.
Put an X on the one that doesn't belong.
Then write the name of the sport that the
other objects belong to.

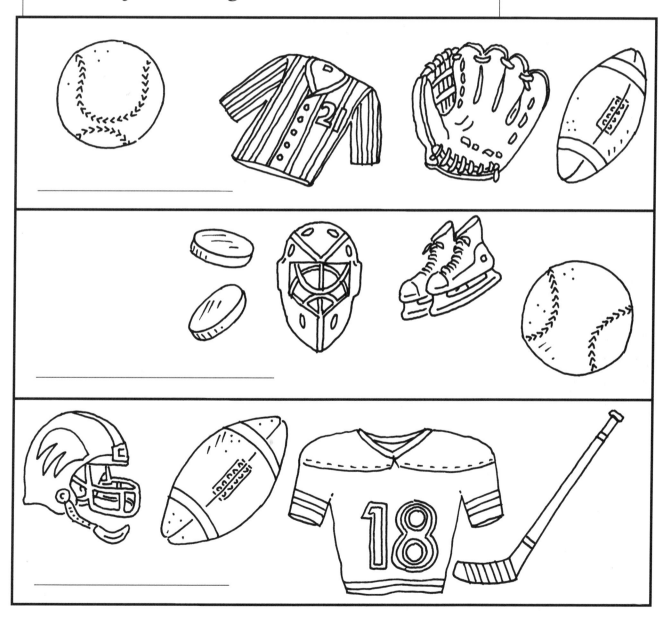

Problem Solving

Identify too much
or too little
information

NAME _____

Too Much or Too Little?

Read each story problem.
Tell if there is too much or too little
information in each problem.
Circle the answer.

Try to solve the
problem. Is there
some information
missing that you
need to solve it?
Is there extra
information you
didn't need?

1. Matt wants to buy a new hockey stick. He has
    $10. Can he buy the stick?

    too much information   too little information

2. The Hawks have blue uniforms. They scored 2
    goals on Monday. They scored 2 goals on
    Tuesday. They scored 4 goals on Friday. How
    many goals did they score in all?

    too much information   too little information

3. Brian went to the hockey game. He bought a
    hot dog for $1.25 and a hot chocolate. How
    much did he spend?

    too much information   too little information

NAME_____

Picture It

Can you finish the story?
Read each story.
Then write and draw to finish the story.

There were 10 apples on the tree.

___ apples were picked.

___ apples are left.

There were 15 apples.

___ apples were eaten.

___ apples are left.

There were 4 pies.

___ pies were eaten.

___ pies are left.

Here's a hint. The last picture should have less things than the first picture.

Awesome! Now cut out your puzzle piece. Tape or glue it in place on page 64.

Check Yourself: Now go back and check your drawings. Count again. Did you draw the right number?

Around the House: Make up a subtraction story problem about something at your house. Draw a picture to show what happened.

Grade 1

27

NAME _____

Help Randy

The *question* helps you know what to do.

How many in all?
ADD
How many more?
SUBTRACT
How many less?
SUBTRACT

Randy has to count the animals.
But he doesn't know if he should add or subtract.
Read each problem.
Then circle Add or Subtract to show Randy what to do.
The first one is done for you.

1. There are 18 impalas in the game park. There are 12 giraffes. How many more impalas are there than giraffes?

   18 – 12 = 6 more impalas than giraffes

   Add   (Subtract)

2. There are 12 monkeys in the game park. 5 of them are babies. How many monkeys are adults?

   Add   Subtract

3. There are 15 lions lying in the shade. 3 more lions are sleeping in the sun. How many lions are there in all?

   Add   Subtract

4. There are 11 flamingos near the lake and 3 in the grass. There are 4 more flamingos flying. How many flamingos are there in all?

   Add   Subtract

NAME_____

Fix the Robot

The math robot is broken!
Some of its answers are not right.
Read each problem.
If the answer makes sense, circle YES.
If it doesn't, circle NO.

Be sure to read each question carefully! Would you add or subtract? Should the answer be bigger or smaller than the numbers you start with?

1. There were 500 people at the football game. There were 200 other people at the basketball game. How many people went to the games in all?

    Answer: 502
    Does the answer make sense?   YES   (NO)
    because 500 + 200 = 700

2. The Reds scored 13 points in the first half of the game. They scored 12 points in the second half. How many points did they score in all?

    Answer: 55
    Does the answer make sense?   YES   NO

3. Jim had a hot dog at the game. It cost $2.00. He bought a drink for $1.00 and some peanuts for $1.00. How much did Jim spend in all?

    Answer: $4.00
    Does the answer make sense?   YES   NO

4. Jane spent $3.00 on snacks. She gave the food seller $10.00. How much change did she get back?

    Answer: $11.00
    Does the answer make sense?   YES   NO

NAME _____

Missing Numbers

Read each problem.
Write the missing number in the box.
Match the number with the letter in the code.
Write the letter on the line at the bottom of the page.
When you're done, you'll have the answer to the riddle.

4 + ☐ = 6

Use subtraction to find the missing number.
6 − 4 = 2, so
4 + 2 = 6.

1. 5 + ☐ = 10

2. 6 + 7 = ☐

3. ☐ − 9 = 7

4. 2 + ☐ = 11

5. ☐ + 2 = 6

Code
4 = R
5 = O
16 = D
9 = E
13 = L

Riddle: What is something we all get every day?

Answer: _____ _____ _____ _____ _____
            1   2   3   4   5

NAME

Art Sale

Each member of the Art Club had $1.00 to spend at the art sale.
Read what each member bought.
Then look at the prices.
Write a number sentence to show how much each member spent.
The first one is done for you.

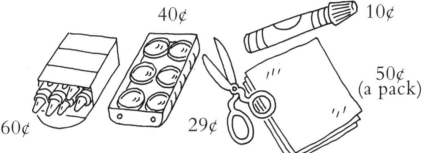

40¢   10¢

60¢   29¢   50¢ (a pack)

A *number sentence* can help you think about a problem.

Good job! Now cut out the puzzle piece. Glue or tape it in place on page 64.

1. Lee bought paints and crayons.

   40¢ + 60¢ = $1.00

2. Ann bought scissors and a marker.

   _____

3. Kelly bought 2 packs of paper.

   _____

4. Bill bought crayons and 4 markers.

   _____

5. Sally bought a pack of paper and 5 markers.

   _____

NAME _____

Number Hunt

Numbers are everywhere!
Look at this picture.
Circle each three-digit number you find.

A 3-digit number, such as 356, has three numerals.

Around the House: Look inside and outside your home for 3-digit numbers. Draw pictures that show where you found them.

NAME_____

Name That Number

Play Name That Number. Here is how:
1. Toss three pennies onto the gameboard. Use the numbers you landed on to make a new number.
2. Write down the new number on another piece of paper.
3. Read the number.
4. Put the numbers in a different order.
5. Read the new number you made.
6. Play again.

0	1	2	3
4	5	6	7
8	9	0	1
2	3	4	5
6	7	8	9

This number—387—is three hundred eighty seven.

Good game! Now cut out your puzzle piece. Glue or tape it in place on page 64.

NAME _____

Who's Who at the Zoo

Help Ziggy find his way at the zoo.
Follow the map.
Then help him remember the order in which
he saw each animal.
The first one is done for you.

Follow the path.
Read the names
of the animals.
Write the
numbers in order
next to each name
on both pages.

ENTRANCE

SEAL 1

POLAR BEAR

PENGUINS

MONKEYS

ZEBRAS

ELEPHANT

GIRAFFE

HIPPO

LIONS

CROCODILE

1. The __seal__ was the first animal Ziggy saw.

2. The second animal was the _____.

3. The _____ were the third animals.

4. The _____ were the fifth animals.

5. The silly _____ were the seventh animals.

6. The eighth animals were roaring _____.

7. Tenth was the _____.

34

NAME_____

Ziggy told his friend Zack some things about the animals he saw.
But, it's a big zoo and Ziggy is confused.
Write on each line whether Ziggy's statement is TRUE or FALSE.

Numbers that tell order are called *ordinal numbers*.

When counting order, begin counting like this: first, second, third, fourth, fifth...

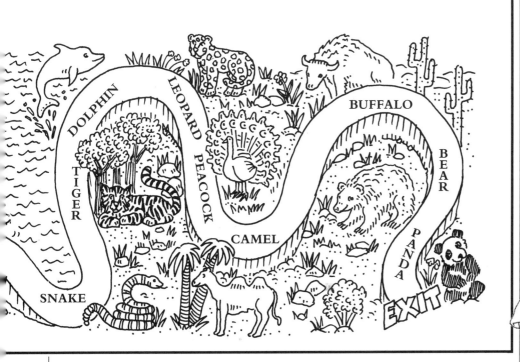

1. The seventeenth animal has two bumps. _____

2. The thirteenth animal lives in the water. _____

3. The sixteenth animal has a big horn. _____

4. The fifteenth animal is a bird. _____

5. The nineteenth animal has black spots. _____

6. The eleventh animal is orange with black stripes. _____

NAME _____

Odd or Even?

If you have none left over, the number is even. If you have one left over, the number is odd.

Excellent! Cut out your puzzle piece. Glue or tape it in place on page 64.

**Count the things in each box by 2s.
Write the answers to the questions.**

1. How many hats are in the box? _____

   Is 6 even or odd? _____

2. How many pencils are in the box? _____

   Is 7 even or odd? _____

3. How many baskets are in the box? _____

   Is 9 even or odd? _____

4. How many ice cream cones are in the box? _____

   Is 4 even or odd? _____

Check Yourself: Did you have an extra pencil and an extra basket?

NAME_____

It's Almost There

Nina likes to collect things.
Help her find out about how many of each
thing she has.
Round each number to the nearest tens.
Circle the right answer.
One is done for you.

To round to the nearest tens, look at the ones place. If the number is less than 5, round down. If it is more than 5, round up.
12 is close to 10.
17 is close to 20.

1. Nina has 19 buttons.
   19 is close to   10   (20)   30

2. Nina has 14 rings.
   14 is close to   10   20   40

3. Nina has 42 shells.
   42 is close to   40   50   20

4. She has 78 flowers.
   78 is close to   70   90   80

5. She has 64 cards.
   64 is close to   50   60   70

6. Nina has 52 books.
   52 books is close to   50   60   100

Around the House: Count the number of books in your room. Are there close to 20, 90, or more?

NAME _____

Riddle Time

Can you solve a riddle?
Do the addition problems.
Then find each sum in the box.
Write the letter that goes with it on the line
to answer the riddle.
The first one is done for you.

Don't forget!
Rename if you
have to.
If you get more
than 9 ones,
rename as tens. If
you get more than
9 tens, rename as
hundreds.

Riddle: What gets wetter the more it dries?
Answer: <u>A</u> ___ ___ ___ ___ ___
1   2   3   4   5   6

1.   14
    + 36
     50

2.   125
    + 136

62	=	L
131	=	O
202	=	E
261	=	T
50	=	A
145	=	W

3.   108
    + 23

4.   124
    + 21

5.   175
    + 27

6.   37
    + 25

NAME

Bee Hive Jive

Help each swarm of bees find the right hive.
Do the problem that goes with each swarm.
Find the answer in a hive.
Draw a line to match the swarm with the hive.

1.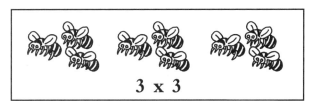

   3×3

    12

2.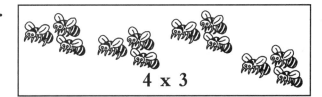

   4×3

    10

3.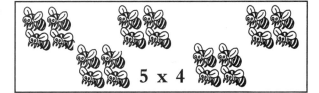

   5×4

    9

4.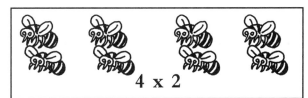

   4×2

   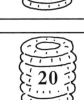 20

5.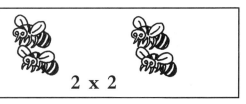

   2×2

    4

6.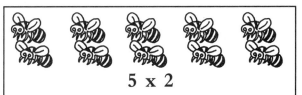

   5×2

    8

If you need help multiplying, add the sets, or count the bees!

Bee-autiful work! Now, get busy with your puzzle piece. Put it in place on page 64.

NAME _____

Party Time

There will be 4 kids at Harold's party. Help him figure out how to share things equally with his friends.
Read the sentences and follow the directions.

Remember! There are 4 kids. Each one should get the same number of things.

1. Harold has 4 party hats.
Draw circles around the hats to show how many each kids gets.

2. Harold has 8 party favors.
Draw circles around the party favors to show how many each kid gets.

3. Harold has 12 cookies.
Draw circles around the cookies to show how many each kid gets.

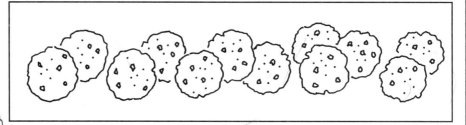

NAME_____

Three in a Row

Write the time under each clock.
Then find three clocks in a row that tell time
in order from early to late.
Draw a line through each row you find.
The rows go across, down, or on a slant.
The first one is done for you.

Here's help: skip count by 5s to find the time after the hour.

It's 9:15!

8:00

8:25

10:15

Check Yourself: Did you find four sets of three clocks in a row?

Around the House: Look around your house.

How many clocks can you find?_____ Write what

time it is now. _____

NAME _____

Toni's Day

The pictures show what Toni does in one day.
The clocks show when Toni does them.
Draw a line to match each picture with the
clock that shows the right time.
The first one is done for you.

The letters *AM*
show that
something
happens in the
morning.
The letters *PM*
show that
something
happens in the
afternoon or
evening.

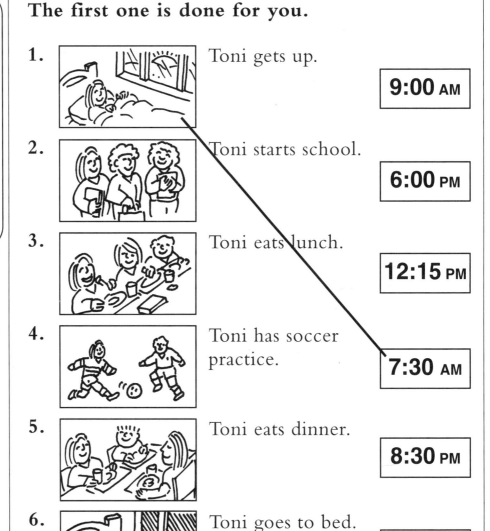

1.   Toni gets up.   **9:00 AM**

2.   Toni starts school.   **6:00 PM**

3.   Toni eats lunch.   **12:15 PM**

4.   Toni has soccer
     practice.   **7:30 AM**

5.   Toni eats dinner.   **8:30 PM**

6.   Toni goes to bed.   **3:30 PM**

NAME_____

Thinking Time

Read each problem.
Draw hands on the clock to answer the
question.

1. The movie starts at 2:00. It is
2 hours long. What time is
the movie over?

2. The picnic ends at 4:00.
It takes 45 minutes to get
home. What time will we
get home?

3. Marty got to the library at
1:30. He stayed a half-hour.
What time did he leave?

To get somewhere
on time, think
about what time
you need to be
somewhere. Then
count back the
time it takes you
to get there.
That's when you
need to leave.

Check Yourself: Go back and read each problem
again. Look at the clock. Count ahead or count back.
Was your answer right?

Around the House: Look at a clock in your house.

What time is it now? _____

What time will it be in 1 hour?_____

NAME _____

Temperature Time

Read each story.
Then read the temperature on the thermometer.
Write the temperature on the line.
One is done for you.

Read a thermometer just like a number line on its side. Most thermometers skip count by 2s.

1. Joe read the thermometer outside his window. He ran back to get his gloves and hat. It is ___**30°**___ .

2. 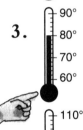 It was 62°. Then it got dark, and the temperature went down 10°. Now it is _____ .

3. 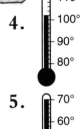 Jim wants to go swimming. His mom said he may go if it is above 75°. It is _____ .

4. 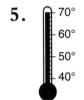 Tanya has a fever. Her dad takes her temperature. It reads _____ .

5. Sam's mom is feeling cold. She turns up the heat. Soon the temperature is _____ .

Around the House: Use a thermometer to check the temperatures around your house.

44

NAME_____

Yard Time

Get a timer and a yardstick or a tape measure. Figure out the answers to these questions. Write your measurements in feet or yards. Work alone or get a friend to time you.

1. How far can you walk in 15 seconds? Mark the starting point. Then count to 15 as you walk. Now mark your ending point. Measure the distance from starting point to ending point.

   Write it here. _____

2. How far can you skip in 15 seconds? Mark the starting point, skip and count, then mark the ending point. Measure the distance.

   Write it here. _____

3. How far can you hop on 1 leg in 15 seconds? Mark the starting point, hop and count, then mark the ending point. Measure the distance.

   Write it here. _____

4. How far can you run in 15 seconds? Mark the starting point, run and count, then mark the ending point. Measure the distance.

   Write it here. _____

Around the House: Name some items in your house that can be measured in yards. Then measure them.

1 yard = 3 feet
1 yard = 36 inches

It's puzzle time again! Cut out the piece and place it on page 64. Can you guess what it is yet?

NAME _____

Milk Measure

Here's a chart that will help:

1 pint = 2 cups

1 quart =
2 pints = 4 cups

1 gallon =
4 quarts = 8 pints =
16 cups

Can you figure out how much milk the Leche family drinks?
Read each problem.
Write the correct number on the line.
Use the chart to help you.

1. On Monday, Linda Leche drank 4 cups of milk. How many quarts did she drink in all?

   4 cups =_____ quart(s)

2. On Tuesday, Larry Leche drank 3 pints of milk. His brother Leo drank 5 pints. How many quarts did they drink in all?

   8 pints =_____ quart(s)

3. On Wednesday, Leroy Leche drank 18 cups of milk. How much did he drink in gallons and quarts?

   18 cups =_____ gallon(s) and _____ pint(s)

   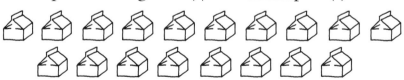

4. On Thursday, Julie Leche drank 2 quarts of milk. How many cups did she drink?

   2 quarts =_____ cup(s)

46

NAME_____

Meter Measure

Help Nina decide which measurement she
should use.
Look at each thing Nina is measuring.
Then circle the measurement.

|___| 1 cm
centimeter   meter

1.
centimeter   meter

2.
centimeter   meter

3.
centimeter   meter

4.
centimeter   meter

One *meter* equals
100 *centimeters*.

Way to measure
up! Now put the
puzzle piece in
the right spot on
page 64.

Around the House: Use a ruler with centimeters
to measure small things in your room.

NAME _____

Liter Aid

less than a liter   about a liter   more than a liter

A *liter* is used to measure liquids, such as milk, and cooking ingredients, such as sugar.

Larry is making lemonade.
Read the sentences.
Look at the pictures.
Circle the things he needs.

1. Larry needs 3 liters of water.
   How much water should he use?

2. Larry needs more than 1 liter of lemon juice.
   How much lemon juice should he use?

3. Larry needs $\frac{1}{2}$ liter of sugar.
   How much sugar should he use?

Around the House: Make your own lemonade. Ask a grown-up for help. Take 1 liter of water. Add $\frac{1}{3}$ liter of lemon juice. Add $\frac{1}{6}$ liter of sugar. Stir well. Add ice. How many liters of lemonade do you have? Now drink a glass!

NAME_____

Box Work

Boris works at the box factory.
He folds up the boxes.
Help Boris match each pattern with the box
it will make.
Draw a line from the pattern to the correct
box.

1.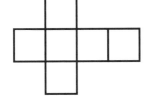

a.

2.

b.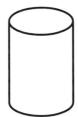

3.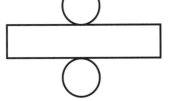

c.

4.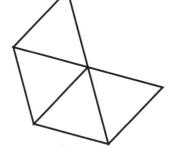

d.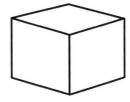

NAME _____

Break the Code

Look at each row of shapes.
Circle all the polygons.
Solve the riddle by writing each letter in order.
The first one is done for you.

What did Molly say when her parrot flew away?

This is a *polygon.*
A polygon is a closed shape with straight sides.

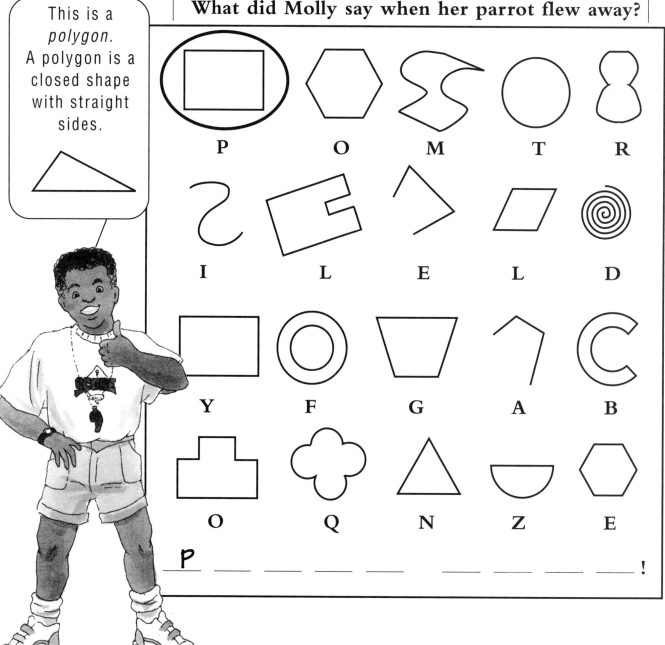

P   O   M   T   R

I   L   E   L   D

Y   F   G   A   B

O   Q   N   Z   E

P _ _ _ _ _ _ _ _ _ _ _ !

NAME _____

Sharp Eyes

How sharp are your eyes?
Look at the first figure in each row.
Then find another figure in the row that is
the same shape and size.

Psst! The shapes may be turned a different way.

You're sharp! Here's your puzzle piece for page 64. Go for it.

1.

2.

3.

4.

NAME _____

Folding Fun

Fiona is making paper shapes.
She folded her paper in half.
Then she cut out a shape on the fold.
What did she see when she unfolded the paper?
Finish the drawings to show what she saw.
The first one is done for you.

Want help? Use a small mirror. Hold it on the fold so you can see both sides.

1.

2.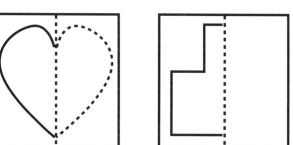

3.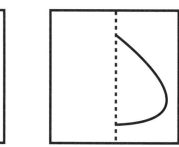

4.

5.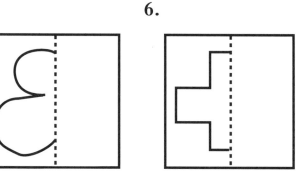

6.

Around the House: Fold paper and cut out a shape on the fold. Can you guess what it will look like before you unfold the paper?

NAME_____

Party Time

Help Tim decide if he has the right number
of things to share at his party.
Read each question.
Write a yes or no answer.
If the answer is yes, show how to share the
things equally.
Circle the right amount for each friend.

Equal means the
same amount.

Use beans or
pennies to try to
make equal sets
of each number.

1. 4 friends like cupcakes. Can 4 friends share

   these cupcakes equally? _____

2. 2 friends like lollipops. Can 2 friends share these

   lollipops equally? _____

3. 3 friends want to play with cars. Can 3 friends

   share these cars equally? _____

Check Yourself: Did you make equal groups? Did
you make the right number of groups?

NAME _____

Favorite Sports

Maya found out her friends' favorite sports. She made a graph to show the information. Look at her graph. Then answer the questions.

Here's how to read the graph: Find the sport name. Then count the figures in the column to find the number of friends who like it best.

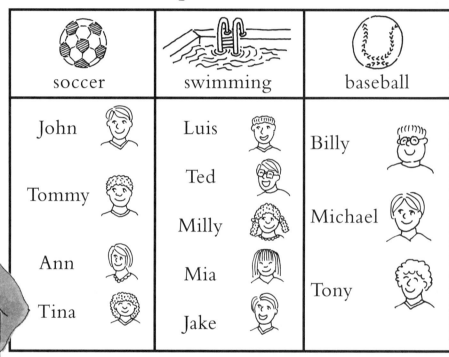

soccer	swimming	baseball
John	Luis	Billy
Tommy	Ted	
	Milly	Michael
Ann	Mia	
Tina	Jake	Tony

1. How many friends like soccer best? _____
2. How many friends like swimming best? _____
3. How many more friends like swimming than soccer? (Hint: You have to subtract for this answer.) _____
4. Should Maya have a party at a park where friends can play both baseball and soccer? Or at a pool where they can swim? Why?

_____

_____

NAME_____

Bird Watch

Kimi is using a table to keep track of the birds she sees.
Use the information below to help her finish the table.
Make a tally mark / for each bird.
Then use the table to answer the questions.

On Monday, Kimi saw 3 blue jays and 2 sparrows.
On Tuesday, Kimi saw 2 blue jays and 1 sparrow.
On Wednesday, Kimi saw 4 sparrows.
On Thursday, Kimi saw 1 blue jay.
On Friday, Kimi saw 1 blue jay and 2 sparrows.

A *table* is a chart that helps you read information easily. Read it from left to right and from top to bottom.

Days of the week	blue jays	sparrows
Monday		
Tuesday		
Wednesday		
Thursday		
Friday		

1. On which day did Kimi see the most blue jays?

   _____

2. On which day did Kimi see the most sparrows?

   _____

3. On which day did Kimi see the most birds?

   _____

4. How many birds did Kimi see in all? _____

NAME _____

Pick One, Which One?

When you flip a coin, how do you know whether you'll get heads or tails? Get a coin, and try this activity. Then fill in the chart, and answer the questions.

A *table* is a kind of chart. It makes information easy to read.

1. Flip a coin ten times. Record your flips in the chart. For each flip, write H if you got heads. Write T if you got tails.

flip 1	
flip 2	
flip 3	
flip 4	
flip 5	
flip 6	
flip 7	
flip 8	
flip 9	
flip 10	

2. How many times did you flip heads? _____

3. How many times did you flip tails? _____

4. Think about the next time you flip a coin. Is it more likely to be heads or tails? Or are your chances of flipping either about the same?

Around the House: Try this activity with two coins. What are your chances of flipping two heads? What about two tails? What about a heads and a tails?

NAME_____

Read the Code

Find the secret message. Here is how.

1. Look at each number pair at the bottom of the page. Then look at the graph.
2. Find the first number in the pair along the bottom of the graph. Put your finger on it.
3. Find the second number along the left side. Put a finger from your other hand on it.
4. Slide your two fingers up from the bottom and across from the left. Find the place where the numbers meet.
5. Read the letter. Write it on the line above the number pair. One is done for you.

Way to go! Glue or tape your piece in place on page 64. Is the puzzle coming together yet?

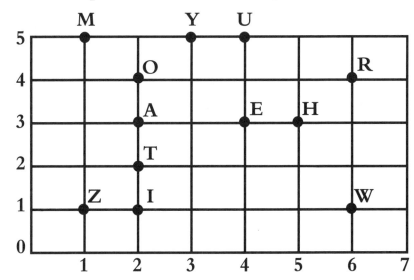

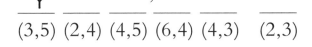

$\underline{\text{Y}}$ $\underline{}$ $\underline{}$, $\underline{}$ $\underline{}$ $\underline{}$
(3,5) (2,4) (4,5) (6,4) (4,3) (2,3)

$\underline{}$ $\underline{}$ $\underline{}$ $\underline{}$ $\underline{}$ $\underline{}$ $\underline{}$ $\underline{}$!
(1,5) (2,3) (2,2) (5,3) (6,1) (5,3) (2,1) (1,1)

NAME _____

Toy Store

Ravi, Mia, Stu, and Ann want to buy toys. Help them figure how much they will spend. But don't add. Make a good guess instead! Circle each answer.

To make good guesses, round off to the closest number.
41¢ is close to 40¢.
48¢ is close to 50¢.
40¢ + 50¢ = 90¢

1. Ravi wants to buy the boat and the truck. He will spend

   more than 70¢   less than 70¢

2. Mia wants to buy the bear and the robot. She will spend

   more than 90¢   less than 90¢

3. Stu wants to buy the action figure and the book. He will spend

   more than 70¢   less than 70¢

4. Ann wants to buy the plane and the train. She will spend

   more than $1.00   less than $1.00

Around the House: Get prices from a newspaper ad. Make a good guess about how much they would cost all together. Add to check your guess.

NAME_____

Find the Clues

Help Inspector Dawg solve these problems.
Read each one.
Circle the number of steps Inspector Dawg
should take to solve it.
Then draw a line from the problem to the
correct answer.

1. Fido had 10 bones.
   He buried 1. He gave 1 away.
   How many does he still have?

   $10 - 1 = 9$ $9 - 1 = 8$

   1 step   (2 steps)

2. Fifi had 6 bones.
   She buried 4 bones.
   How many does she have left?

   1 step   2 steps

3. Spot had 4 bones.
   Then he got 5 more bones.
   How many bones does he
   have now?

   1 step   2 steps

4. Wags had 3 bones.
   He lost 1 and gave 1 away.
   How many bones does he
   have now?

   1 step   2 steps

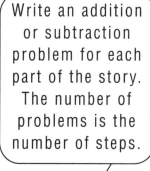

Write an addition
or subtraction
problem for each
part of the story.
The number of
problems is the
number of steps.

Hot dog!
Now cut out your
piece. Put it in
place on page 64.

NAME _____

Seesaw Fun

Count the birds on each side of the seesaw.
Write the number on the line below each side.
Then write >, <, or = to finish each sentence.
The first one is done for you.

Use these signs.
> more than
< less than
= equals
Remember, the point goes toward the smaller number.

1.

<u>3</u> > <u>1</u>

2.

_____ _____

3.

_____ _____

4.

_____ _____

5.

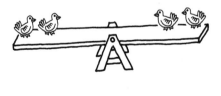

_____ _____

6.

_____ _____

NAME_____

Help the Computer

The computer isn't working right!
It printed the following number sentences.
But it left out some numbers.
Write the missing number in each box.

1. 4 + ☐ = 12

2. ☐ − 8 = 8

3. ☐ + 3 = 6

4. 9 + ☐ = 19

5. ☐ − 7 = 6

6. 5 + ☐ = 10

7. ☐ − 2 = 6

8. 18 + ☐ = 25

9. 19 − ☐ = 9

10. ☐ + 12 = 18

Remember:
addition and
subtraction are
opposites.
Knowing one
helps you know
the other.

NAME _____

Sox Match

Billy needs help matching his socks.
Read the number sentence in each sock.
Find a number sentence on another sock that
is equal.
Draw a line to connect the two socks.

You can add or
multiply in any
order.

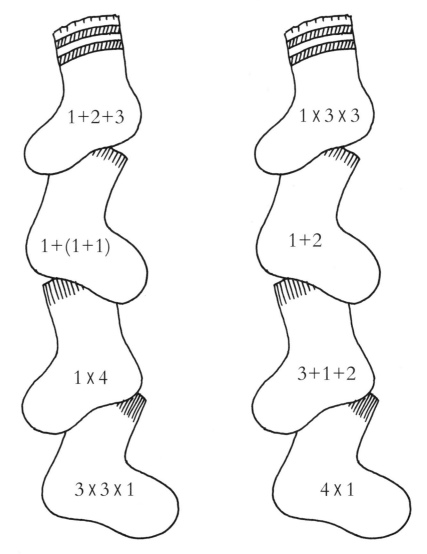

1+2+3

1+(1+1)

1 X 4

3 X 3 X 1

1 X 3 X 3

1+2

3+1+2

4 X 1

Check Yourself: Add or multiply. Does each pair
you connected have the same answer?

62

NAME_____

Math Machines

Read the numbers on the shapes that fell out of the machine.
Can you figure out the numbers that fell into the machine?
Write the numbers in the matching empty shapes.

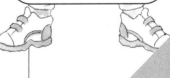

Pssst! Here's a hint. Put the answers through the machine backwards. Do the opposite of what it says.

You're now a math machine! Pop your final piece into place! Congratulations!

Check Yourself: When you think you know the answer, put the number through the machine. Did you get the right answer?

Puzzle

Here's where you glue or paste the puzzle pieces you cut out. When you put them all in place, you'll see your secret message.

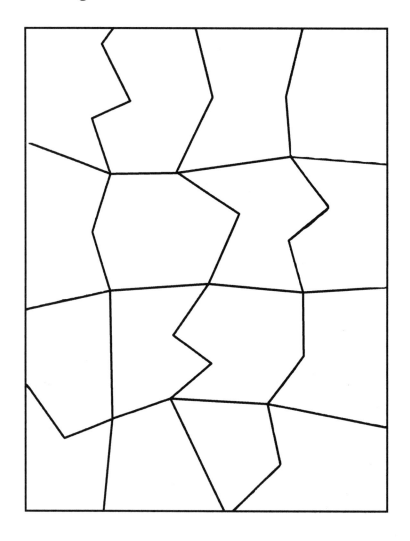

Answers

Page 1
Answers will vary.

Page 2
1. 6
2. 13, 16
3. 18, 20, 21, 22
4. 24, 25, 27, 29

Page 3
Answers will vary.

Page 4
1. 12, 14, 16, 18, 20
2. 20, 25, 30, 35, 40
3. 30, 40, 50, 60, 70

Page 5
1. ◇ 9
2. ☐ 12
3. △ 15
4. ◯ 16
5. ☆ 18

Page 6
1. Greg
2. Eloise
3. Ian
4. Zoe

Page 7
Math is fun

Page 8
1. 21
2. 32
3. 15
4. 11
5. 11
6. 21
7. 32
8. 92
9. 10
10. 22

Page 9
2. 4
3. 4
4. 6
5. 2
6. 3
7. 2
8. 1
9. 8

Page 10
2. 4+4=8
3. 3+3=6
4. 2+2+2+2+2=10
5. 2+2+2+2+2+2=12

Page 11
2. C
3. B and D
4. 5:30
5. 2:00

Page 12
Amy has 57¢.
Jenny has 90¢.
Tad has 36¢.
Jenny has the most money.

Page 13
Answers will vary. Sample answer:
30¢ (robot) + 32¢ (basketball) + 25¢ (ice skates) = 87¢

$1.00 − 87¢ = 13¢

Page 14
1. 90°
2. 62°
3. 35°
4. 15°

Page 15
Answers will vary.

Page 16
1. 9 cm long
2. 2 cm wide, 6 cm long
3. 1 cm wide, 3 cm long
4. 2 cm long, 3 cm wide

Page 17

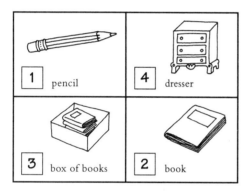

1. pencil, book, box of books
2. pencil
3. pencil, book
4. book

Page 18
Answers will vary.

Page 19
Drawings will vary.

Page 20
1. ◯
2. □
3. △
4. ▭
5. ⬠

Riddle Answer: A comb

Page 21
2. bead with smile, bead with frown, bead with mouth open
3. heart, heart, heart
4. rectangular bead, rectangular bead, rectangular bead

Page 22

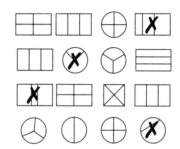

Page 23

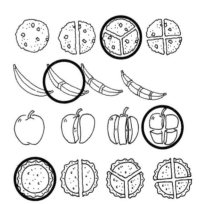

Page 24

1. 7
2. rabbits
3. dogs
4. snake
5. Graph should show 1 more cat.

Page 25

sports: baseball, hockey, football

Page 26

1. too little information
2. too much information
3. too little information

Page 27

1. 6 apples were picked. 4 apples are left. Child's drawing should show 4 apples on the tree.
2. 4 apples were eaten. 11 apples are left. Child's drawing should show 11 apples on the table.
3. 2 pies were eaten. 2 pies are left. Child's drawing should show 2 pies on the table.

Page 28

2. Subtract
3. Add
4. Add

Page 29

2. no
3. yes
4. no

Page 30

1. 5
2. 13
3. 16
4. 9
5. 4

Riddle answer: older

Page 31

2. 29¢ + 10¢ = 39¢
3. 50¢ + 50¢ = $1.00
4. 60¢ + 10¢ + 10¢ + 10¢ + 10¢ = $1.00 or 60¢ + 40¢ = $1.00
5. 50¢ + 10¢ + 10¢ + 10¢ + 10¢ + 10¢ = $1.00 or 50¢ + 50¢ = $1.00

Page 32

Page 33

Answers will vary.

Page 34

2. polar bear
3. penguins
4. zebras
5. monkeys
6. lions
7. crocodile

Page 35

1. False   4. True
2. True   5. True
3. False   6. False

Page 36

1. 6, even   3. 9, odd
2. 7, odd   4. 4, even

Page 37

2. 10   5. 60
3. 40   6. 50
4. 80

Page 38

2. 261
3. 131
4. 145
5. 202
6. 62

Riddle answer: a towel

Page 39

1. 9   4. 8
2. 12   5. 4
3. 20   6. 10

Page 40

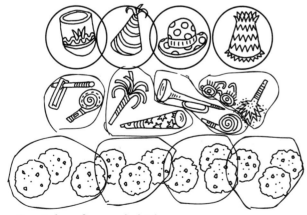

1. 1 hat for each kid
2. 2 favors for each kid
3. 3 cookies for each kid

Page 41

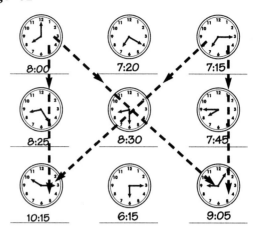

Page 42

2. 9:00 A.M.
3. 12:15 P.M.
4. 3:30 P.M.
5. 6:00 P.M.
6. 8:30 P.M.

Page 43

1. 4:00   2. 4:45   3. 2:00

Page 44

2. 52°
3. 80°
4. 102°
5. 70°

Page 45

Answers will vary.

68

Page 46

1. 1 quart
2. 4 quarts
3. 1 gallon and 1 pint
4. 8 cups

Page 47

1. meter
2. meter
3. centimeter
4. centimeter

Page 48

1.

2.

3.

Around the House: 1½ liters

Page 49

1. d
2. c
3. b
4. a

Page 50

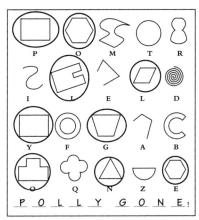

Page 51

1. third figure
2. third figure
3. second figure
4. fifth figure

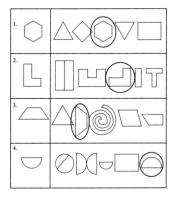

Page 52

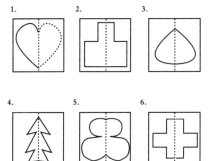

Page 53

1. yes

2. no

3. yes

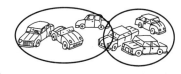

Page 54

1. 4
2. 5
3. 1
4. The best place for a party would be at the park because, if you add the number of people who like soccer to the number of people who like baseball, it is greater than the number of people who like swimming.

Page 55

Days of the week	blue jays	sparrows
Monday	///	//
Tuesday	//	/
Wednesday		////
Thursday	/	
Friday	/	//

1. Monday
2. Wednesday
3. Monday
4. 16

Page 56

Answers will vary.

Page 57

Message: You're a math whiz!

Page 58

1. more than 70¢
2. less than 90¢
3. less than 70¢
4. more than $1.00

Page 59

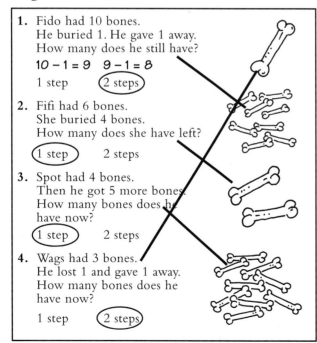

1. Fido had 10 bones.
   He buried 1. He gave 1 away.
   How many does he still have?
   10 − 1 = 9   9 − 1 = 8
   1 step   (2 steps)

2. Fifi had 6 bones.
   She buried 4 bones.
   How many does she have left?
   (1 step)   2 steps

3. Spot had 4 bones.
   Then he got 5 more bones.
   How many bones does he have now?
   (1 step)   2 steps

4. Wags had 3 bones.
   He lost 1 and gave 1 away.
   How many bones does he have now?
   1 step   (2 steps)

Page 60

2. 5 < 7
3. 6 = 6
4. 4 < 5
5. 2 = 2
6. 3 = 3

Page 61

1. 8
2. 16
3. 3
4. 10
5. 13
6. 5
7. 8
8. 7
9. 10
10. 6

Page 62

The following socks match:
1 + 2 + 3 and 3 + 1 + 2
1 + (1 + 1) and 1 + 2
4 + 3 + 1 and 4 + 4
2 X 1 X 2 and 4 X 1
3 X 3 X 1 and 1 X 3 X 3

Page 63

Machine 1: star 14; triangle 7; diamond 21
Machine 2: circle 26; square 9; triangle 15

70

How Do You Foster Your Child's Interest in Learning?

In preparing this series, we surveyed scores of parents on this key question. Here are some of the best suggestions:

- Take weekly trips to the library to take out books, and attend special library events.

- Have lots of books around the house, especially on topics of specific interest to children.

- Read out loud nightly.

- Take turns reading to each other.

- Subscribe to age-appropriate magazines.

- Point out articles of interest in the newspaper or a magazine.

- Tell each other stories.

- Encourage children to write journal entries and short stories.

- Ask them to write letters and make cards for special occasions.

- Discuss all the things you do together.

- Limit TV time.

- Watch selected programs on TV together, like learning/educational channels.

- Provide project workbooks purchased at teacher supply stores.

- Supply lots of arts and crafts materials and encourage children to be creative.

- Encourage children to express themselves in a variety of ways.

- Take science and nature walks.

- Teach children to play challenging games such as chess.

- Provide educational board games.

- Supply lots of educational and recreational computer games.

- Discuss what children are learning and doing on a daily basis.

- Invite classmates and other friends over to your house for team homework assignments.

- Keep the learning experiences fun for children.

- Help children with their homework and class assignments.

- Take trips to museums and museum classes.

- Visits cities of historical interest.

- Takes trips to the ocean and other fun outdoor locations (fishing at lakes, mountain hikes).

- Visit the aquarium and zoo.

- Cook, bake, and measure ingredients.

- Encourage children to participate in sports.

- Listen to music, attend concerts, and encourage children to take music lessons.

- Be positive about books, trips, and other daily experiences.

- Take family walks.

- Let children be part of the family decision-making process.

- Sit down together to eat and talk.

- Give a lot of praise and positive reinforcement for your child's efforts.

- Review child's homework that has been returned by the teacher.

- Encourage children to use resources such as the dictionary, encyclopedia, thesaurus, and atlas.

- Plant a vegetable garden outdoors or in pots in your kitchen.

- Make each child in your family feel he or she is special.

- Don't allow children to give up, especially when it comes to learning and dealing with challenges.

- Instill a love of language; it will expose your child to a richer thought bank.

- Tell your children stories that share, not necessarily teach a lesson.

- Communicate your personal processes with your children.

- Don't talk about what your child did not do. Put more interest on what your child did do. Accept where your child is at, and praise his or her efforts.

- Express an interest in children's activities and schoolwork.

- Limit TV viewing time at home and foster good viewing habits.

- Work on enlarging children's vocabulary.

- Emphasize learning accomplishments, no matter how small.

- Go at their own pace; People learn at different rates.

- Challenge children to take risks.

- Encourage them to do their best, not be the best.